Old Florida

Florida's Magnificent Homes, Gardens, and Vintage Attractions

Steve Gross and Sue Daley

Introduction by Patrick Smith

RIZZOLI
NEW YORK

First published in the United States of America in 2003
by Rizzoli International Publications, Inc.
300 Park Avenue South
New York, NY 10010
www.rizzoliusa.com

2005 2006 2007/ 10 9 8 7 6 5 4 3

Front cover: the former Hotel Ponce de León
(now Flagler College), St. Augustine
Page 2: El Jardin, Coconut Grove
Page 3: Mermaid statue,
Weeki Wachee Springs Park, near Tampa
Page 5: The Orange Shop, Citra
Page 6: Lion statue at Ca d'Zan dock,
John and Mable Ringling Museum, Sarasota

Captions by Elizabeth Johnson
Design by Judy Geib and Aldo Sampieri
Printed in China

ISBN: 0-8478-2563-9
Library of Congress Control Number: 2003104982

Old Florida

Contents:

Introduction

Traveling throughout Florida is like watching the changing patterns and colors of a kaleidoscope—you never know what will come up next. The state is a mixture of Old World and New, the sublime and the bizarre, and a lot of "Florida Cracker" in between.

Time was when the roads in Florida were lined with small souvenir stands offering stuffed baby alligators, conch shells, plastic paperweights with a Florida scene inside (usually a cabbage palm), and pink plastic flamingoes. But no more. All this has vanished, but much of Old Florida is still there, and it has been captured vividly by Steve Gross and Sue Daley.

Over the centuries since the Spanish first came here, Florida has attracted an eclectic mix of immigrants inside one state: Spanish, British, French, Greek, German, Italian, Minorcan, Cuban—and the list goes on and on and on, including those rugged pioneers of the eighteenth and nineteenth centuries who trickled in after the Civil War, eventually establishing cattle ranches and orange groves. All of this is reflected in homes elsewhere, some in cities and some off the beaten path.

Let's start on the west coast, in Cedar Key. You do not "pass through" Cedar Key going elsewhere. You either go there deliberately, or you never see it at all. It is located on a two-lane road twenty-six miles off Highway 19/98, and the road dead-ends there. Once you arrive you will have taken a step backward in time. The original pioneer-days charm is still there.

Cedar Key was once a lumber town, and during the Civil War, it supplied salt for the Confederate army. Later on it turned to seafood as its prime industry. Today its quaint streets are lined with small shops, galleries, and restaurants serving some of the freshest seafood found in Florida, especially local oysters. My favorite breakfast in Cedar Key is fried mullet and grits. Don't knock it till you've tried it, because you might become hooked.

The Island Hotel in Cedar Key, a "one of a kind" pre–Civil War structure, was built with seashell tabby with oak supports. Originally a general store and post office, it is now a small thirteen-room hotel.

Just a bit down the road from here you come to one of Florida's original theme parks, Weeki Wachee Springs, featuring an underwater theater where real live "mermaids" perform daily. Truth be known, as many visitors (men) probably enjoy seeing those beautiful, young "mermaids" perform as others are charmed by the gardens and a spring flowing 170 million gallons of water a day.

Travel south and *Old Florida* takes you to Tarpon Springs, which was once known as the "Sponge Capital of the World," an industry established by Greeks. The small town has preserved its Greek heritage, and the old sponge docks are still there. Nearby are souvenir shops, restaurants serving authentic Greek food (and *real* Greek ouzo), and

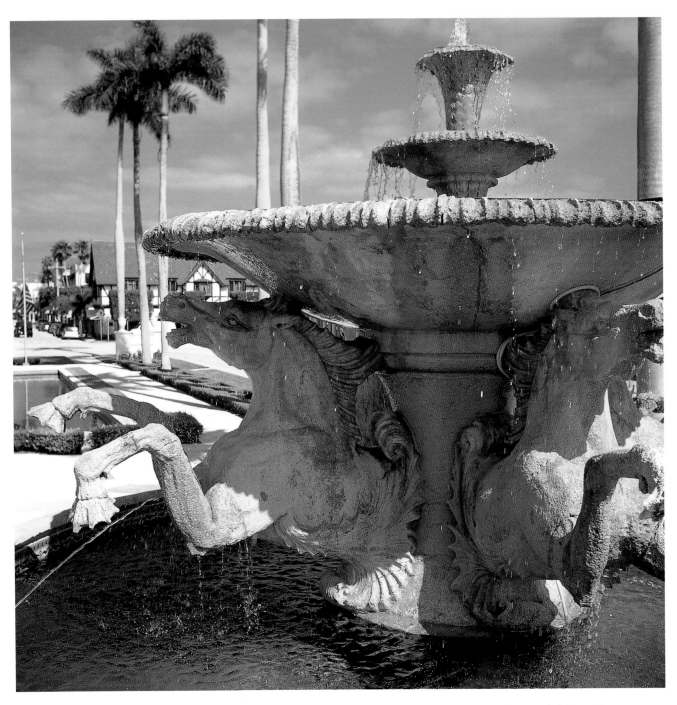

Palm Beach's Memorial Fountain was designed by one of Florida's best-known architects, Addison Mizner. The fountain's basin is supported by rearing horses.

the Spongerama Exhibit Center. The town has never been commercialized, and it remains basically as it was long ago.

A hop away is St. Petersburg, one of the state's original "retirement cities" with numerous shuffleboard courts, beautiful streets, and the exotic Sunken Gardens; then across Tampa Bay is Tampa and Ybor City, both representing Old Florida.

The center of nineteenth-century Tampa social life was the Tampa Bay Hotel, built in the late 1880s by Henry B. Plant. In 1898, when troops assembled in Tampa to be shipped to Cuba for the Spanish-American War, the hotel housed Army officers, their wives, and newspaper correspondents headed for Cuba. In this group was Lt. Colonel Theodore Roosevelt and his Rough Riders. The old hotel is now a museum on the campus of the University of Tampa.

Across town, Ybor City was the home of Cuban cigar makers, and parts of it resemble old Havana. Located here too is one of Florida's most famous restaurants, the Columbia. *Old Florida* also takes you to other historic places in the Tampa area.

For a glimpse of how the super-wealthy once lived, we find Ca d'Zan in Sarasota, built by John Ringling of circus fame. This Venetian Gothic mansion staggers the mind, and *Old Florida* takes you inside this fabulous estate.

South of Ft. Meyers, past the winter home of notables Thomas Edison (included in this book) and his neighbors Henry Ford and Harvey Firestone, we come to a genuine

"offbeat" part of Old Florida, the Koreshan Settlement at Estero, which was built by religious zealots who believed humans lived inside the earth. They established here all they needed, including membership cottages, a bakery, sawmill, sewing room, and vegetable gardens. Much of it is still there today and is a state historic site open to the public. It is not known, however, if those Koreshan pioneers ever made contact with their inside-earth brothers.

Next stop on this introduction tour is the once isolated fishing village of Everglades City, which is located where Highway 29 ends after it crosses Highway 41, nearby the Big Cypress Swamp. Everglades City is the northern waterway entrance to the Florida Everglades National Park and its Ten Thousand Islands area, a fisherman's paradise. Over the centuries the waterways through the islands have seen the likes of—you name it—Indians, Spanish explorers, pirates, outlaws, rum runners, drug runners, hermits, commercial fishermen, and those modern-day adventurers who make canoe trips all the way from Everglades City down to Flamingo on the southern tip of the park.

It is here we find the rustic Rod and Gun Club, once a private retreat for men who loved to do what the name suggests: fish and hunt. The lodge is no longer private, and its facilities are open to the public. The dining room in the lodge is an excellent place to enjoy what is, to me, the most

Simple, rural, Peniel Baptist Church, in Palatka, has the drop-lap siding and corner boards typical of the period before the Civil War. One thing, however, sets this specimen apart: evangelist Billy Graham was ordained here, and he was baptized in a nearby lake.

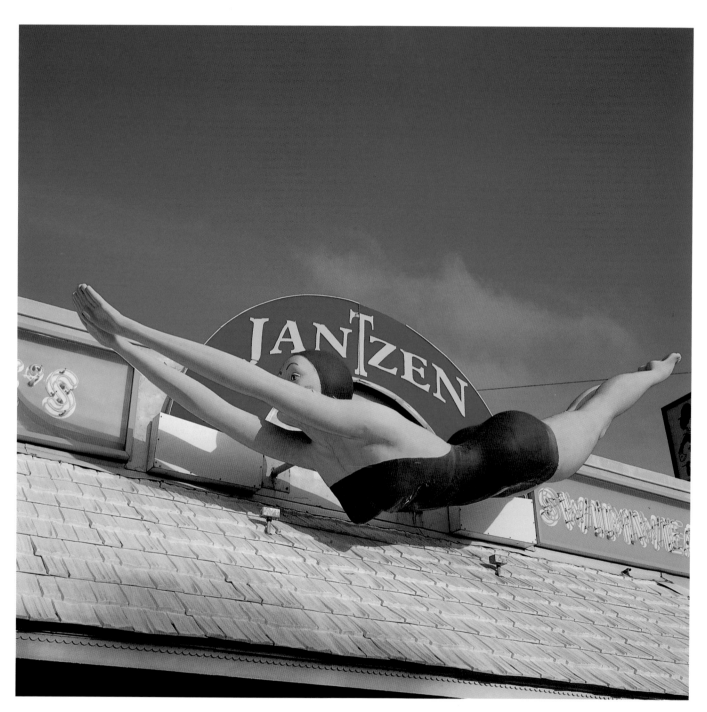

A memorable sign near the historic boardwalk and pier in Daytona Beach advertises swimsuits for bathing beauties.

delectable thing harvested in local Everglades City waters: stone crab claws.

Cross over a small bridge and you're on Chokoloskee Island, and here you will find a surviving relic of Old Florida, the Smallwood Store, once a pioneer-era general store and a trading post for Seminole Indians. If anything will transport you backward in time, this old building will. It is crammed with merchandise that many people today have never seen, and it is open to the public as a museum.

The Seminoles came to the store in wooden dugout canoes and were dressed in original Seminole attire that resembled all the colors of a rainbow. Stand outside the store today, close your eyes, and in your mind's eye you can see them coming, their dugouts laden with things to trade. Or else you might see them fade into the horizon.

From here we take a giant leap to the upper reaches of the east coast, to Fernandina Beach and Amelia Island, a bubbling cauldron of Florida history. Just south of here, on Fort George Island, is the remains of the Kingsley Plantation, built in the early 1800s in the time of slavery. The slave quarters are still there, as is the main plantation house.

.Traveling through historic Jacksonville and then south, we come to St. Augustine, where it all began. The oldest continuous settlement in the United States, St. Augustine has relics going all the way back to the sixteenth century.

One could spend weeks just wandering the streets and alleys of this city, seeing something fascinating along each block, and *Old Florida* includes an extensive mix of St. Augustine historic sites.

Move on down to Daytona Beach, which once billed itself as "The World's Most Famous Beach"—and it probably was, year-round anyway. It was an early mecca for sunbathers, swimmers, and gawkers, and also for race-car drivers and fans. Back in the old days, races were held on the beach itself, which in places was packed as hard as concrete. Sir Malcolm Campbell drove his "Bluebird" down the sands of Daytona Beach on March 7, 1935, at a speed of 282.018 miles per hour.

My wife, Iris, and I spent our wedding night at Daytona Beach in 1948, and we have memories of those small "tourist court"–type motels that lined the beach. A few are left, and this book takes you there.

Just south of here, at Port Orange, is the Gamble Place, a retreat built by James Gamble in 1907. One of the unusual attractions here is a tiny log cabin, built in 1940, that resembles the dwarfs' cabin in *Snow White and the Seven Dwarfs*.

One of the most popular Old Florida attractions was located at Vero Beach, the McKee Jungle Garden. Opened to the public in 1932, the eighty-acre garden contained one of the world's largest collections of palms, native plants, orchids, and lilies. It was laced with paths and ponds. After being closed for several years, part of the garden was restored and is now open again as the McKee Botanical Garden.

Travel seventy miles inland from here, to Lake Wales, and you find what I have always called "a balm for the soul," the Bok Tower Sanctuary, containing beautiful gardens and a 205-foot tall marble and coquina belltower housing a sixty-bell carillon. When the bells ring forth each day it is like music raining down from heaven. It has a tranquilizing effect.

Take another giant leap down to Coral Cables, and something located here has stayed in my memory since I saw it for the first time as a young kid in 1933: the Venetian Pool. We were on a family vacation trip, and when we chanced upon that pool, my young eyes popped out. I wanted to jump right in, clothes and all. It was a fantasy land. It is still there today and is just as fascinating as it was to a young boy almost seven decades ago. You will visit it in *Old Florida*.

There are two houses in this book, former homes of famous writers, that are "Cracker houses." One is the Cross Creek home of Marjorie Kinnan Rawlings, and the other is the Wabasso house of Laura (Riding) Jackson.

Marjorie Rawlings purchased her small house and orange grove in 1926 and moved there from New York. For ten years she had been a journalist at newspapers in Kentucky and New York, and had tried to write fiction but failed. When she moved

to Cross Creek she had decided to quit writing altogether, in disgust at not being able to get anywhere. Her only intent at Cross Creek was to grow oranges. Over the years she did grow oranges, but her main crop was novels and short stories.

Mrs. Rawlings' first Florida novel, *South Moon Under*, was published in 1933, and this was followed in 1935 by *Golden Apples*. Her 1939 novel, *The Yearling*, won the Pulitzer Prize. *When the Whippoorwill*, a collection of her scrub-country short stories, was published in 1940, and her nonfiction book, *Cross Creek*, in 1942. Her final novel, *The Sojourner*, this one set in New England, was published in 1953.

My first visit to Mrs. Rawlings' home at Cross Creek was in 1947, and I went back as often as possible, several times shortly after her death in 1953. The home is basically the same as it was when she first moved there. It is now preserved as a state park.

The Florida life of Laura (Riding) Jackson is a different story, except for the style of the house. She was a renowned avant-garde poet of the 1920s and lived the literary life both in this country and then in Europe. She returned to New York in 1939 and renounced poetry. In 1941 she married Schuyler Jackson, *Time* magazine poetry critic, and they moved to Wabasso where they purchased a small 1890 frame house and an eleven-acre citrus grove.

The Jacksons raised citrus for a gift fruit business and worked together at night on a new type of dictionary. Schuyler

In the Cedar Key village of commercial fisherman and artists, many tin-roofed, weather-beaten, vernacular houses are found. This one has wooden awnings, fishing floats, and an old church pew for porch seating.

The Vesta Newcomb cottage at the Koreshan Settlement was a residence for members.
Besides operating a general store, the utopian Koreshans also ran a publishing house, manufactured furniture,
and provided electricity to Estero when much of the county was still using candlelight.

died in 1968, leaving Laura alone. Until 1989 (almost fifty years), Laura lived in her home without electricity. After her death in 1991, the house was vandalized and threatened with demolition, then in 1992 a private foundation was created to preserve it. In 1994 the house was moved from a mile west and sits today on the grounds of the Environmental Learning Center in Wabasso.

Laura (Riding) Jackson was awarded the Bollingen Prize for poetry in 1990, and she is recognized in *Who's Who in 20th Century Literature* as "the most consistently good woman poet of all time." Why would such a literary genius quit writing poetry and choose to spend the major part of her life in virtual seclusion in an isolated Cracker house without electricity? Who knows but her, but it is a part of the Old Florida mystique.

Final stop on this brief introduction tour is Merritt Island, where I have lived since 1966. It really is an island, located between the Indian and Banana rivers. Kennedy Space Center sits on a section of north Merritt Island.

If ever there was an example of Old Florida clashing with New Florida, this is it. The first-known inhabitants of Merritt Island, pre-1513, were the Ais Indians. When the Spanish established St. Augustine they named the present Indian River the River of Ais. The Ais lived along the river from north of Melbourne to south of Ft. Pierce. In the mid-1700s, the Ais became extinct—simply vanished from the earth, and no one really knows why.

Many things happened in the area over the next century, and many footprints were left behind, but it was not until shortly after the Civil War that pioneer settlers trickled onto Merritt Island to establish permanent homesteads. They came to raise cattle, pineapples, and sugar cane. Later, citrus became king.

Before the Kennedy Space Center and the "Gateway to Space," most of Merritt Island was citrus groves, and life moved at a slow pace. The space program changed that. Some orange groves remain, but many have been replaced with houses. There is a photo in this book taken along the old North Tropical Trail, and it gives you an idea of what all of this place once was. The northernmost part of Merritt Island is now the Merritt Island National Wildlife Refuge, and this wilderness area looks today the same as it did when the Ais were here. It will remain so forever, a part of Old Florida sitting right next door to a place where men left this earth and went to the moon.

There are many fabulous places in *Old Florida* I have not mentioned, but they are there for you to view. If you came to Florida today, and visited each place in this book, it would take weeks, or even longer. Steve Gross and Sue Daley have made it easy for you. All you have to do is sit back in a comfortable recliner, start turning pages, and experience an intriguing trip through one of the most diverse areas on earth.

Enjoy!

The St. Petersburg Shuffleboard Club was founded in 1924 and grew to become the world's largest. Many of the sport's champions were based at the club, once known as the Mirror Lake Club, and it played a role in the development of tourism and leisure in the area. Long associated with Florida, shuffleboard goes back to the fourteenth and fifteenth centuries, when it was first played on ships.

A patriotic citrus-packing barn still stands in an orange grove on Merritt Island. Residents of Merritt Island, home to some of the state's oldest citrus groves, worked almost exclusively in the citrus industry until the arrival of the space age and nearby Cape Canaveral lured them away.

Amelia Island
Ft. George Island

St. Augustine

Cross Creek

Daytona Beach
Port Orange

Cedar Key

DeBary

Cape Canaveral

Tarpon Springs

Tampa

Lake Wales

Vero Beach

St. Petersburg

Sarasota

Lake Okeechobee

Fort Myers

Palm Beach

Estero

Fort Lauderdale

Everglades City
Chokoloskee Island

Miami   Miami Beach
Coral Gables

Homestead

Built around 1798 for a Spanish merchant named Andres Ximenez,
this house originally held a general store and tavern on the ground floor and the
Ximenez family home upstairs. In 1830, a widow named Margaret Cook bought the property
and turned it into a boardinghouse—one of the few acceptable business ventures for
nineteenth-century women. Eight guestrooms held up to twenty-three visitors, including the
speculators, sea captains, and invalids who flowed into Florida at the time. Subsequent
owners—Sarah Anderson followed by Louisa Fatio—remodeled the structure and rented
rooms to wealthy northerners who spent their winters in St. Augustine.

Now a public house museum maintained by the Colonial Dames of America,
the building is preserved as it was during Florida's territorial period, from 1821 to 1845,
when the area's tourism industry began.

Right: With its painted floorcloth and comfortable sofa, this first-floor parlor is
where guests would have relaxed before or after meals with magazines, playing cards,
and a chess table. Mosquito netting hangs across the door to the dining room.

24

Second-floor guestrooms, such as this one, were reserved for single women, couples, and families.
Single men were kept on the first floor. All of the beds were shrouded in mosquito tents, which have been used in Florida since
the eighteenth century. Twists of newspaper, arranged like a bouquet in a vase on the mantel, were used to light fires.

Ximenez-Fatio House, St. Augustine

Reputations of boardinghouses were made in the dining room by the quality of food, or "board."
Meals were served family-style, with the largest meal taken mid-day. Over the table hang two punkah fans
covered in canvas frames with fringed edges.

Ximenez-Fatio House, St. Augustine

ST. AUGUSTINE ALLIGATOR FARM

The St. Augustine Alligator Farm is one of the oldest attractions of its kind and, in recognition of its role in the development of tourism, has been placed on the National Register of Historic Places. In the early twentieth century, a small souvenir shop on St. Augustine Beach featured live alligators for the fascination of tourists. As the popularity of these exotic examples of native Florida wildlife caught on, the owners of the shop expanded and created the South Beach Alligator Farm and Museum of Marine Curiosities in 1909. It was moved to its present location on Anastasia Island in 1920.

Although the farm houses more than 2,700 gators and crocodiles, including representatives of all twenty-three species, it is more than just an alligator farm. It is also a zoological park. Other reptiles and tiny monkeys can be seen, and egrets, wood storks, and tricolored herons nest above the alligator ponds.

27

St. Augustine Alligator Farm

St. Augustine was founded by the Spaniard Don Pedro Menendez de Aviles in 1565, forty-two years before Jamestown, Virginia, making it the oldest permanent European settlement in North America. Although Spain ceded Florida to the English in 1763 (they eventually retook control in 1783), the British newcomers incorporated many elements of Spanish residential architecture into their own style. These holdovers include fronting houses directly onto the street, walled compounds, and cooling loggias. The British brought with them double-hung windows, hipped roofs, and dormers, which can be found on many local eighteenth-century houses.

Left: Time, weather, and the sun have left a rich patina on many buildings in St. Augustine. In the nineteenth century the city became famous as a place whose mild climate could help heal the sick. Ralph Waldo Emerson, who spent the winter of 1827 in St. Augustine recovering from tuberculosis, wrote, "The air and sky of this ancient fortified dilapidated sandbank of a town are really delicious."

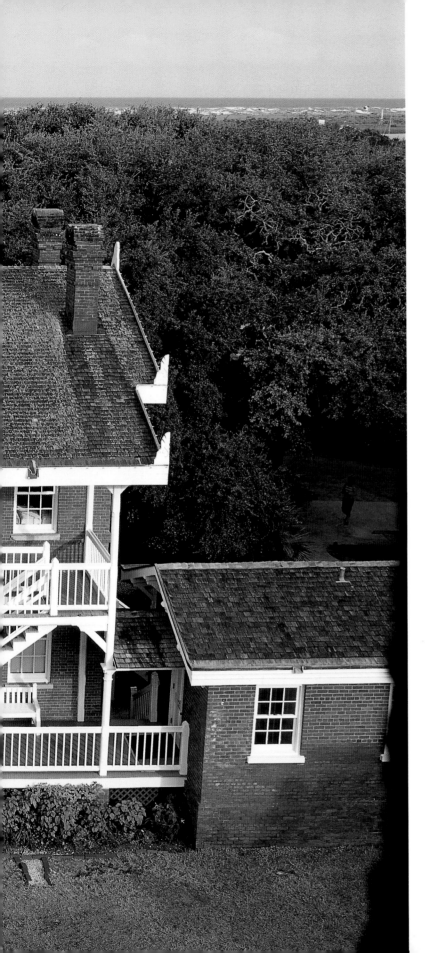

LIGHTKEEPERS' HOUSE
ST. AUGUSTINE LIGHTHOUSE
AND MUSEUM

The current lighthouse in St. Augustine has been protecting sailors since 1874. Constructed of brick, granite, and iron with a black-and-white spiral stripe, it replaced a wooden Spanish watchtower. The lightkeepers' house, seen here with the Atlantic Ocean in the background, was built in 1876 between the lighthouse and the ocean. (The original house was gutted because of a fire in 1970 and rebuilt in 1988.) It housed up to three lightkeepers (a head lightkeeper and two assistants) and their families.

Before electricity, the keepers worked eight-hour shifts to provide service twenty-four hours a day, 365 days per year. In addition to welcoming visitors, sheltering shipwreck victims, painting, and maintaining logbooks, the keepers lit the light every night at sunset. This meant carrying thirty-pound buckets of the fuel—hot lard oil—up more than two hundred stairs. The keeper also had to crank the heavy clockworks system that rotated the lens. Electricity and automation eventually led to the demise of the light-keeper's job, but the lighthouse is still in operation today.

31

HOTEL PONCE DE LEÓN (FLAGLER COLLEGE), ST. AUGUSTINE

As part of the development of St. Augustine into a stylish winter resort, entrepreneur Henry Flagler commissioned young New York architect Thomas Hastings (later a partner in the firm of Carrere and Hastings) to design the Hotel Ponce de León in 1887. Modeled after a Moorish castle, the hotel is adorned with domes, spires, turrets, and fountains. Its interior is decorated with Louis C. Tiffany stained glass, mosaics, and terra-cotta relief. The fashionable hotel was a popular destination and enjoyed success for a number of decades but was eventually sold to Flagler College.

32

Hotel Ponce de León (Flagler College), St. Augustine

The oldest Spanish Colonial house in Florida, the González-Alvarez House in St. Augustine is a National Historic Landmark. The earliest building on the site—a log hut with a thatched roof built in the 1600s—was replaced at the beginning of the eighteenth century by a one-story house. That building, made of a regional limestone of shells and coral called coquina, forms the base of the structure standing today. The wood-frame second story was added during the British period. The complex has been a public museum since 1918.

Left: Spanish kitchens like this one were often housed in separate outbuildings to reduce the threat of fire and to avoid increasing heat in the house. At the González-Alvarez House, the kitchen is in the garden, which is planted with species grown by the house's Spanish, British, and American occupants over the centuries.

Beneath the hand-hewn cedar beams of the ground floor hangs a wall shelf altar with a candle,
rosary, and an image of the Madonna beneath a crucifix. Many Spanish settlers were Catholic,
and their religious influence was brought to the New World.

Right: The tavern room at the González-Alvarez House contains English-style furniture and opens onto
an inner courtyard. Just outside the door, a pumice stone drinking fountain, used to filter water, can be seen.
The filter was brought by the Spanish settlers from the Canary Islands.

González-Alvarez House, St. Augustine

The ground floor depicts Spanish and British lifestyles from the mid-1700s. This room is furnished with Spanish pieces, including a chest and bench. Even the earliest Florida settlers resourcefully managed pests. The charcoal brazier in the center of the room was used not only for heat; its smoke was purposely kept in the house to kill mosquitoes. The food rack above the table swings in order to keep rats from the provisions.

González-Alvarez House, St. Augustine

40

The oldest remaining plantation house in Florida is named after its third owner, Zephaniah Kingsley, who bought Fort George Island and lived in the house from 1814 to 1837. From the rooftop observation deck, which was built for watching vessels approach on St. John's River, much of the Sea Island cotton plantation could be seen.

Kingsley was married to Anna Madgigine Jai, a Senegalese woman he had bought as a slave but freed five years later, in 1811. Following Senegalese tradition, Anna lived in a separate house linked to the main building by a covered walkway that can be seen at the left of this photo. She managed the plantation with her husband and even acquired her own land and slaves. After Florida was purchased by the U.S. in 1821, oppressive racial laws were enacted, and Kingsley, Anna, and their children moved to Haiti.

Kingsley Plantation, Ft. George Island

The ruins of twenty-three slave cabins still stand on the property.
Made of coquina stone with cedar roofs, they were strong and dry. The cabins were laid out in a semicircle to reflect the
arrangement of a traditional African village. The large cabin at the end housed one of the slave drivers.

Kingsley Plantation, Ft. George Island

FISHING BOAT AND DOCK
FERNANDINA BEACH, AMELIA ISLAND

Amelia Island, named for the daughter of
King George II, is a narrow barrier island near the
Georgia-Florida border. Once a thriving port, Amelia
spawned modern shrimping techniques when local
fishermen replaced rowboats and cast nets with
power nets and trawls in the early twentieth century.

42

Fishing Boat and Dock, Fernandina Beach, Amelia Island

PRIVATE RESIDENCE
FERNANDINA BEACH, AMELIA ISLAND

Much of Fernandina's charm today can be traced to Henry Flagler's decision to bypass Amelia Island when he built his railroad along Florida's East Coast. As a result, tourism and modernization went elsewhere, preserving it as a Victorian seaport village. The "Captain's House," as this edifice is known, sits in the Old Town section of Fernandina, where a cluster of houses once owned by fishermen and retired sea captains remains.

Private Residence, Fernandina Beach, Amelia Island

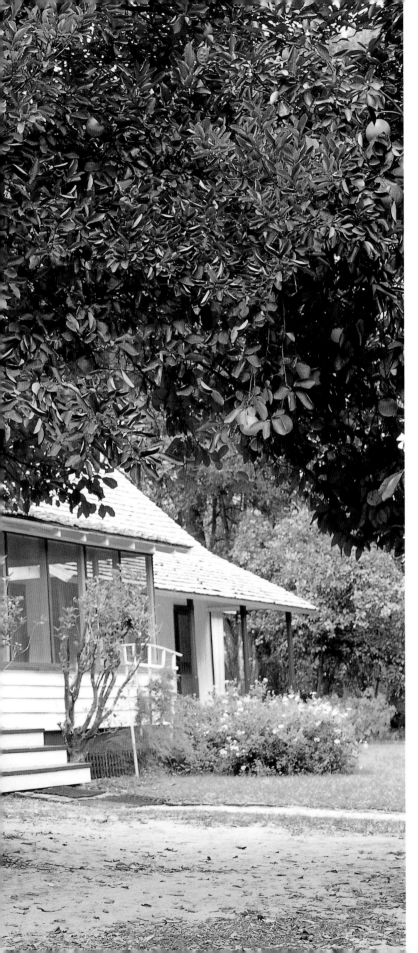

MARJORIE KINNAN RAWLINGS HOUSE, CROSS CREEK

Author Marjorie Kinnan Rawlings lived in this farmhouse from 1928 until her death in 1953. Her novel *The Yearling*, which won the Pulitzer Prize in 1938, is set in the area. Ernest Hemingway, editor Charles Scribner, and other members of the literary world visited her here.

The house, with its still-lived-in look, exemplifies what has come to be known as the Florida "Cracker style"—modest wood-frame homes set on raised blocks, with metal roofs, porches, high ceilings, and lots of strategically placed windows. The style is a vernacular response to the local environmental conditions of intense heat, high humidity, and heavy rains. (The name, once derogatory but now reclaimed, refers to the sound of a whip cracking over wild cattle, which many early Floridians herded.)

47

49

An excellent cook and an avid entertainer, Rawlings once wrote,
"For my part, my literary ability may safely be questioned . . . but indifference to my table puts me into a rage."
Her enthusiastic writings about food prompted her readers to request a cookbook; she responded with
Cross Creek Cookery in 1942.

Marjorie Kinnan Rawlings House, Cross Creek

Rawlings added screens to the porches and used this one for sleeping. Beyond her old car in the carport, her beloved citrus trees are visible from the bed. She grew lemons, grapefruit, tangerines, and numerous types of oranges.

Marjorie Kinnan Rawlings House, Cross Creek

50

Over the years, Rawlings added many improvements to the house, from an indoor bathroom
to a generator and electric lights. She shaded the bare bulbs with painted wooden bowls, as seen here in the living room.

Marjorie Kinnan Rawlings House, Cross Creek

The yard remains much as it appeared in Rawlings's time, with chickens, a vegetable garden, napping cats, and Spanish moss hanging on the clothesline. As Rawlings would say, "It is necessary to leave the impersonal highway, to step inside the rusty gate and close it behind. One is now inside the orange grove, out of one world and in the mysterious heart of another."

Marjorie Kinnan Rawlings House, Cross Creek

THE YEARLING RESTAURANT, HAWTHORNE

This restaurant near Cross Creek opened in 1952, serving visitors from Maine to Miami what it calls "Cracker cuisine," or "anything out of the lakes and woods nearby," including venison, quail, alligator, catfish, and frog legs.

54

The Yearling Restaurant, Hawthorne

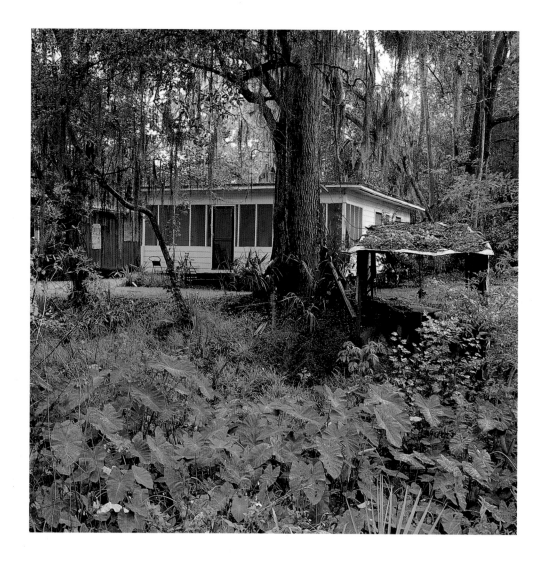

This old fishing camp is in an area of Hawthorne known as "The Creek."
The region's rustic charm and two nearby lakes—Orange Lake and Lake Delancey—
lure outdoor enthusiasts and fishermen, who revel in its slower way of life.

Right: This hidden scenic lookout offers timeless river views and
glimpses of a highway bridge over Cross Creek.

Fishing Camp, Hawthorne

HISTORIC BOK SANCTUARY, LAKE WALES

The Singing Tower at the Historic Bok Sanctuary is a carillon, a musical instrument of enormous cast-bronze bells that are played from a keyboard. Made of coquina stone and marble, the tower features elaborately carved screens and friezes and serves as the focal point of the Bok gardens.

The Historic Bok Sanctuary was the brainchild of Edward Bok (1863–1930), an immigrant from the Netherlands who wanted to create a gift to the American people. Bok came to the United States at age six and went on to become a successful publisher, magazine editor, and Pulitzer Prize winner. He hired Frederick Law Olmsted, Jr., son of the landscape architect who created Central Park, to transform Iron Mountain, the highest point on the Florida peninsula, from a pine-covered sandhill into a lush garden and a sanctuary for birds and wildlife. As part of his master plan, Olmsted designed the reflecting pool that offers visitors their first glimpse of the tower.

Dedicated in 1929 by President Calvin Coolidge, the sanctuary is a National Historic Landmark today.

Historic Bok Sanctuary, Lake Wales

The ground floor of the tower is one vast, open room. Above the fireplace are a map showing the course of the winds and the advice that inspired Bok to create his sanctuary: "Make you the world a bit better or more beautiful because you have lived in it," which is what his grandmother told him when he left Holland as a boy.

Historic Bok Sanctuary, Lake Wales

Left: A moat fifteen feet wide surrounds the tower, whose teak door is covered with brass and depicts scenes from the Book of Genesis. A marching band of native wildlife, including pelicans, herons, and fish, encircles the tower at a height of thirty feet. Edward Bok is buried in a crypt at the base of the tower.

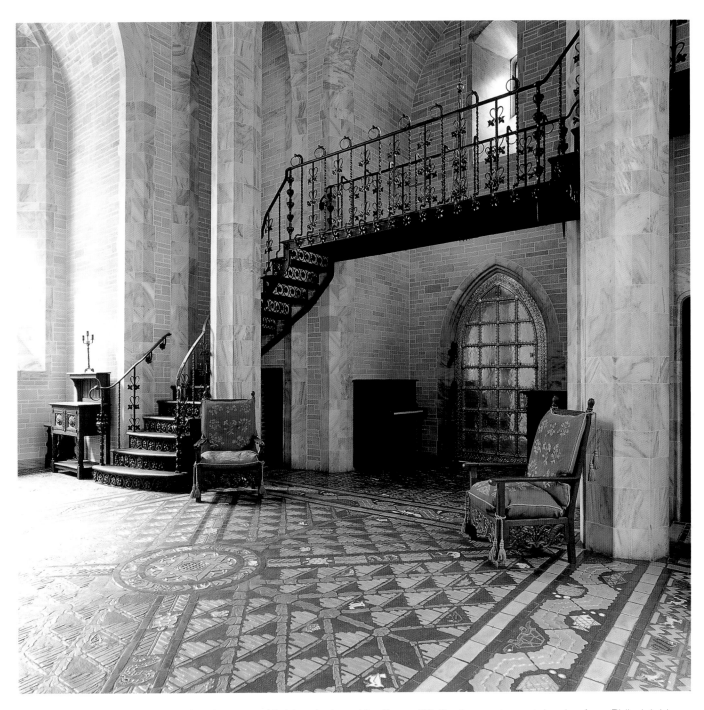

Inside the tower is an ironwork staircase and bridge designed by Samuel Yellin, the master metalworker from Philadelphia who also created the bronze door. Ceramic floor tiles by J. H. Dulles Allen depict aquatic wildlife, from sea snakes and shellfish to turtles and snails.

Historic Bok Sanctuary, Lake Wales

PINEWOOD ESTATE
HISTORIC BOK SANCTUARY
LAKE WALES

This elegant estate adjacent to the Bok Sanctuary was built in the early 1930s as the winter home of Charles Austin Buck, the vice president of Bethlehem Steel. Buck hired William Lyman Phillips—of the firm of Frederick Law Olmsted, Jr., who was transforming the Bok property—to design the grounds. A pioneer in the use of palms and tropical plants that had been previously ignored, Phillips has had a profound influence on the landscaping of Florida today.

Phillips rendered the gardens first and sited the house later in order to dictate a naturalistic flow from garden to house. The house, originally called El Retiro (*retreat* in Spanish), typifies the Mediterranean Revival style, with tile roof, carved woodwork, and elaborate wrought iron. Colorful Cuban tiles, such as those on the bench in the foreground, decorate the house inside and out. The stone courtyard beyond centers around a Spanish frog fountain.

Pinewood Estate, Historic Bok Sanctuary, Lake Wales

67

The living room of Pinewood, like the rest of the house, is furnished with Spanish, French, and Italian antiques. Twist columns, tile-and-wood floors, and thick walls as evidenced in the deep windows recall Latin architecture.

Pinewood Estate, Historic Bok Sanctuary, Lake Wales

68

Cedar Key is a historic fishing village on Way Key,
the largest of the Cedar Key Islands in the Gulf of Mexico.
The main street of this once thriving seaport and rail terminal is lined with
buildings, hotels, and saloons that date back to the nineteenth century.
Long ago, cedar trees covered the island until pencil companies
sawed them down and shipped them north to pencil factories.
A hurricane in 1896 destroyed the sawmills.

Right: The old Cedar Key Seafoods building harkens back to the island's days as
a commercial fishing center. Oysters, sponges, seahorses, and turtles were harvested.
Even today, the area is home to Florida's clam-farming industry.

70

Tarpon Springs, on the Gulf of Mexico, is the "natural sponge capital of the world." Founded in 1876, the town became home to Greek sponge-divers in 1905, when deep-sea diving methods were perfected, enabling them to sponge in deep water. (Before this time sponge was collected by "hooking" in shallow waters in places like Key West.) Today, the town's Greek heritage remains strong, with colorful family-run cafés, bakeries, produce stands, and social clubs. The blue and white buildings on this side street evoke the flag of the residents' homeland.

Right: This well-tended cottage and garden are typical of Tarpon Springs's Greek neighborhoods.

72

One of America's quintessential Victorian resorts, the Moorish-style
Tampa Bay Hotel was built by Henry Plant. Plant, a railroad entrepreneur from Connecticut,
had transformed Tampa from a village into a city when he made it the terminal point for his
rail network. The hotel was an enormous, self-contained paradise, complete with five
hundred guestrooms, a domed dining room, a solarium, tennis, golf, and bird hunting.
Today it is part of the University of Tampa and a time capsule of the Gilded Age,
showing how the hotel appeared to its guests when it opened in 1891.

Henry B. Plant Museum, Tampa

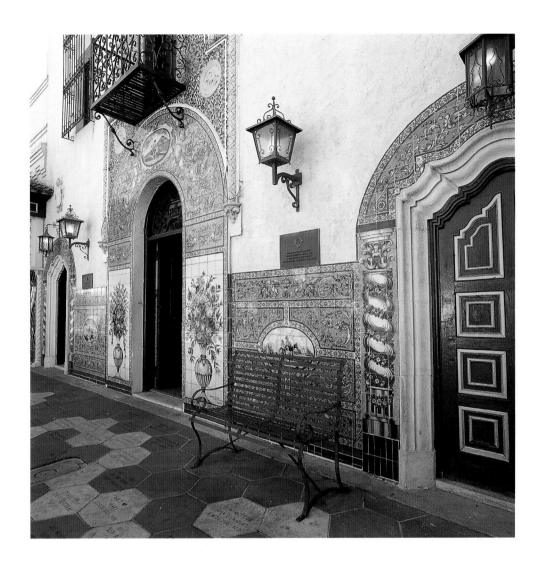

The Columbia is Florida's oldest restaurant and the world's largest Spanish restaurant.
It was founded in 1905 by Casimiro Hernandez, whose family still owns it.
Located where three encampments in the Spanish-American War connected,
it became a watering spot for the Rough Riders and their animals,
including Teddy Roosevelt's horse Texas and dog Cuba.

Ybor City was founded in 1886 by two Cuban exiles who were also cigarmakers, Don Vincent Martinez Ybor and Don Ignacio Haya, who promptly built the largest cigar factory in history. They also brought other cigar manufacturers to the city. Abundant manufacturing jobs attracted Cuban, Spanish, and Italian immigrants, who soon made Ybor City the "Cigar Capital of the World," known for its fine Cuban cigars and producing seven hundred million cigars a year. By the 1950s, its demise was almost complete, as automation and the popularity of cigarettes took over.

At Ybor City's peak, workers lived in shotgun-style casitas, which they could buy from Don Ybor at cost. The Ybor City State Museum has restored three casitas and furnished one of them in a manner typical of the period. The living room is decorated simply with family portraits. Mosquito netting and religious items outfit the bedroom. Today Ybor City is a designated historic district.

Cigar Worker's Casita, Ybor City State Museum, Tampa

TAMPA THEATRE, TAMPA

The golden age of movies lives on in the ornate Tampa Theatre, which has been described as an "Andalusian bonbon." Since its opening in 1926, the theater has shown vaudeville acts, orchestra concerts, war newsreels, and of course movies. Architect John Eberson, designer of many of the country's most ostentatiously elaborate movie palaces, employed his "atmospheric style" here, creating an exotic setting. Tampa Theatre includes grottoes, fountains, and trompe l'oeil moonlit skies. It was also the first public building in Tampa with air-conditioning.

Tampa Theatre, Tampa

The building's "lobby overlook" is open to the main lobby below.
With 1,446 seats in the theater, large circulation spaces were needed
to accommodate patrons before and after shows.

Tampa Theatre, Tampa

78

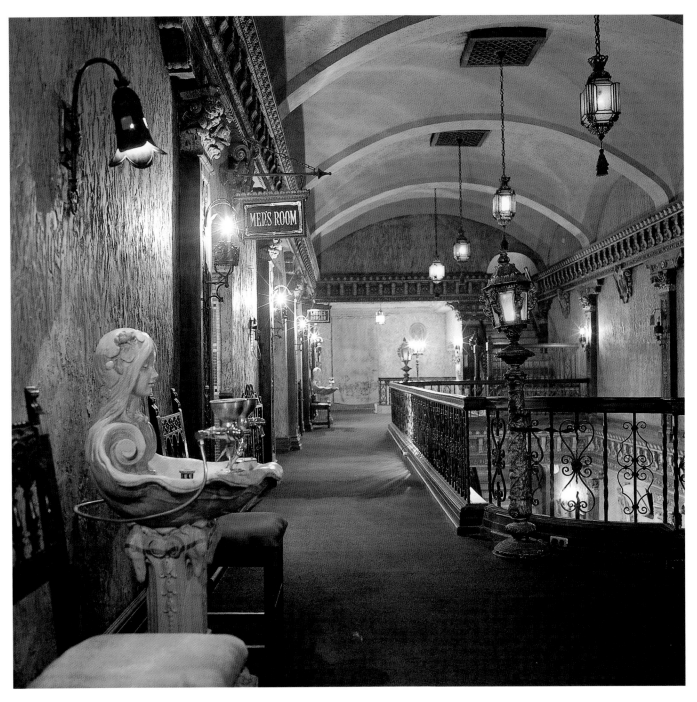

Lavish promenades, such as this one with its shell-shaped water fountains on the mezzanine level,
allow visitors to feel like movie stars themselves. The building, which is on the National Register of Historic Places,
is no museum—it is used regularly for films, concerts, and special events.

Tampa Theatre, Tampa

SUNKEN GARDENS, ST. PETERSBURG

St. Petersburg's Sunken Gardens occupy four acres that were
originally home to a large sinkhole and a shallow lake.
A plumber named George Turner bought the property in 1903 and,
by draining the water with carefully placed clay tiles, created a rich soil ideal for gardening.
By the 1920s local residents were paying a nickel to tour Turner's tropical gardens,
and one of Florida's oldest roadside attractions was born.
Soon a fruit stand, gift shop, and birds and wildlife were added.
This arched red bridge spans one of Turner's many ponds.

Right: Throughout the gardens, which sit fifteen feet below street level,
Turner created a background of green that contrasts and complements every flower.
Visitors meander on colored stone walkways.

Right: The soft rush of a waterfall punctuates the dense foliage of the gardens.
Since 1999 Sunken Gardens has been owned by the city of St. Petersburg,
whose citizens have undertaken a community effort to preserve the historic property.

82

Chilean flamingoes eat by bending their long necks and putting their black bills into shallow water.
Flamingoes were introduced to Sunken Gardens in 1957.

Sunken Gardens, St. Petersburg

CA D'ZAN
JOHN AND MABLE RINGLING MUSEUM
SARASOTA

The King of the Circus and his wife built this Italian Renaissance–style mansion between 1924 and 1926 overlooking the Sarasota Bay. The following year, John Ringling moved the winter quarters of his Ringling Brothers & Barnum and Bailey circus from Bridgeport, Connecticut, to Sarasota. Open to the public, it rapidly became the most visited tourist attraction in Florida.

The couple's thirty-room residence is modeled on the Doge's Palace in Venice. Its name, Ca d'Zan, means "House of John" in a Venetian dialect. Mable had spent years traveling European cities with a Brownie camera, recording ideas for her own home. During their travels, the couple had acquired immense collections of furnishings and art, including the largest group of paintings by Peter Paul Rubens in the world.

84

Ca d'Zan, John and Mable Ringling Museum, Sarasota

The Tower, centered over the house's main façade, was lighted whenever the Ringlings were in residence at Ca d'Zan. From the thirty-one-foot tower, one could survey the vast extent of the property and Sarasota Bay. John Ringling's yacht, the "Zalophus," was moored at a dock in the bay. Mable's gondola was docked opposite the terrace, on a small island that was washed away by a hurricane in 1926.

The Tower's tile details, created by the O. W. Ketcham Terra Cotta Works, include cats, bats, owls, Zodiac symbols, flowers, and marine life.

Ca d'Zan, John and Mable Ringling Museum, Sarasota

In the magnificent court at Ca d'Zan, every surface and furnishing is luxurious. Cypress beams supporting
the thirty-two-foot-high ceiling were painted by Robert Webb, Jr., an apprentice to John Singer Sargent.
Seventeenth-century tapestries hang from the upper gallery. An 1875 French tapestry rug covers marble tile floors.
The chandelier's origins, by comparison, seem humble: it comes from a New Orleans hotel that was torn down.

Ca d'Zan, John and Mable Ringling Museum, Sarasota

The coffers of the ballroom's gilt ceiling are painted with twenty-two vignettes of "dancers of nations."
Keyhole-arched windows recall Islamic architecture.

Ca d'Zan, John and Mable Ringling Museum, Sarasota

Left: In John Ringling's private tap room, the stained glass and wood paneling were taken from the bar of a St. Louis restaurant and customized to fit this space. The heavily veined wood is typical of Art Deco, the height of European style when this house was built.

The Ringlings and their guests played billiards and cards in the Play Room.
The artist Willy Pogany painted the ceiling murals, featuring John and Mable Ringling dressed in Venetian carnival costumes dancing among their pets.

Ca d'Zan, John and Mable Ringling Museum, Sarasota

Dozens of dramatic sculptures populate the gardens. The Ringlings had a taste for exotic plants and trees, including banyans like the one seen behind this sculpture.

Ca d'Zan, John and Mable Ringling Museum, Sarasota

HISTORIC SMALLWOOD STORE
CHOKOLOSKEE ISLAND

Chokoloskee Island is part of the "10,000 Islands" along the western edge of the Everglades. Inhabited by Native Americans for more than two thousand years, the island had its first white residents in the late nineteenth century. Most of them were hunters seeking plumes, hides, and furs. An enterprising resident named Ted Smallwood opened his Smallwood Store and Indian Trading Post in 1906, cornering the market on general goods and fur trading. Smallwood also ran the post office out of the store. Each day when the mailboat arrived, he notified islanders by blowing a conch shell horn.

The store stayed in business until 1982, after it was already on the National Register of Historic Places. Roughly 90 percent of the stock at the time remained in the store, and Smallwood's granddaughter recently reopened the store as a museum.

95

Historic Smallwood Store, Chokoloskee Island

As the center of commerce in this remote area, the store filled many needs,
from cooking supplies and hardware to shoe cobbling.

Historic Smallwood Store, Chokoloskee Island

Mangrove trees ring the water's edge near the Smallwood Store (on stilts to the right). For many years, the store served both white frontiersmen and Seminole Indians. This building dates to 1916, after the original store was destroyed in a hurricane. The murder of Edgar J. Watson—inspiration for Peter Matthiessen's novel *Killing Mr. Watson*—took place near here in 1910.

Historic Smallwood Store, Chokoloskee Island

ROD AND GUN CLUB, EVERGLADES CITY

The Rod and Gun Club, with genteel yellow-and-white-striped awnings, is now a rustic waterfront lodge and old-fashioned restaurant. The building occupies the site of the house of W. S. Allen, the first permanent white settler in the area and the founder, in 1864, of Everglades City. A tycoon named Barron G. Collier bought it in 1922 and turned it into a private sportsmen's club, where he entertained such dignitaries as John Wayne and Presidents Roosevelt, Truman, and Eisenhower.

Collier made Everglades City the headquarters for his Tamiami Trail road-building company in 1923. Linking Tampa with Miami, the trail crossed the state through the swamplands. Collier was captivated by the untamed beauty of the area's grassy waters and invested millions in the trail. The county was named in his honor.

Rod and Gun Club, Everglades City

The walls of the lobby are paneled in red cypress and decorated with guns, fishing rods, and trophies.
A stuffed bobcat is just one example of taxidermy on view.

Rod and Gun Club, Everglades City

The two originally identical houses that make up Thomas Edison's retreat
were, in keeping with the owner's career as a creative inventor, designed with his
recommendations. Built in sections in Maine, the two prefabricated houses were brought
to Florida by schooners and assembled on site. Called Seminole Lodge, the retreat
served as a winter home for Edison and his second wife, Mina, until her death in 1947.
The second building served as a guesthouse.

Edison first visited Fort Myers in 1885 and bought riverfront property for his home
and small laboratory the same year. The gardens originally contained unusual hybrids,
bred by Edison for their products or byproducts, which he used in his scientific work.
During the earlier years of his visits to the house, Edison experimented with
the process of carbonizing bamboo to be used as light-bulb filaments.

Right: The Tea House sits next to a swimming pool built by Edison in 1910 for
use by his children and guests. Built of Edison Portland Cement, one of his patents,
the pool is one of the first modern swimming pools in Florida.

Thomas Edison House, Fort Myers

The living room of Edison's home is furnished with wicker pieces and opens onto deep, cooling verandas. Edison designed the electric chandeliers, called "electroliers," which were handmade of a combination of metals, porcelain, and glass.

Thomas Edison House, Fort Myers

A telephone equipped with an intercom system tops the desk in the Edisons' bedroom.
The room has been preserved much as Mina Edison left it.

Edison spent untold hours in his laboratory. He once announced, "I owe my success to the fact that I never had a clock in my workroom." He even saw his deafness as a blessing in this regard, as it allowed him to work undisturbed. Edison and his team raised goldenrod in the estate's experimental gardens in attempts to find a domestic source of rubber.

Thomas Edison House, Fort Myers

110

The Koreshans were a utopian communal religious group who moved from Chicago to Estero in 1894 to establish their "home grounds." Led by their founder, Dr. Cyrus Teed, who assumed the biblical name Koresh, the Koreshans practiced a form of Christianity that prized education, vocational training, celibacy, equality of the sexes, and the value of each member leading a productive life.

Most of the buildings in the settlement are gone, but among the twelve remaining is the bakery, seen here inside and out. The large facility could produce up to six hundred loaves per day for the members and customers at the Koreshan store. The second floor of the bakery contained four dormitory rooms.

Many Koreshan members lived in simple, unpainted cottages like this one. Throughout the settlement, paths were paved with crushed seashells that provided a firm walking surface and reflected light in the evening.

The Koreshans cleared the grounds of thick mangroves to make room for fruit and nut trees, vegetable gardens, and aesthetic gardens to nourish the spirit. They grew some vegetables commercially, and sold homemade jams and jellies to the local community.

113

Koreshan Unity Settlement, Estero

114

This packing house on the property that once belonged to James N. Gamble,
the son of the cofounder of Procter and Gamble, was built around 1907.
It supported a surrounding orange grove that included Mandarin orange and
kumquat trees, the fruits of which Gamble often shipped to friends and relatives
around the country. Although little of the grove remains today,
the modest pine-and-cedar barn still stands.

Citrus Packing House, Gamble Place, Port Orange

WITCH'S HUT, GAMBLE PLACE

Sharing the Gamble Place grounds is a group of whimsical "enchanted forest" buildings inspired by the 1937 Disney animated film *Snow White and the Seven Dwarfs*. The structures—the Witch's Hut and Snow White Cottage—are full-size replicas of the film's sets and were commissioned by Judge Alfred Nippert, Gamble's son-in-law. The Witch's Hut, seen here, was built from a hollow cypress tree that was roofed and set on a stone foundation.

Nippert sent his carpenter, Ernie Whidmeier, to watch the film over and over in order to create architectural drawings. Still not satisfied, Nippert eventually obtained the original animation cels from Disney to reference.

116

Witch's Hut, Gamble Place

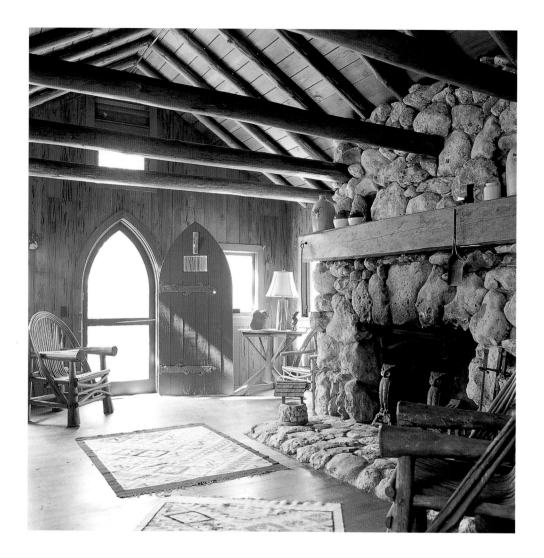

118

Nippert was so charmed by the *Snow White* movie that he decided to build a replica
of the cottage as a playhouse for his nieces. Recognizable from the celluloid original is the
heavy pointed-arch door with strap hinges, the overscaled fireplace, and the
owl andirons. Reconsidered, for practical reasons, were the thatched roof and earthen
walls. Upstairs in the cabin lie seven little beds with inscribed headboards.
Cardboard cutouts of the characters adorn the stairs.

Snow White Cottage, Gamble Place

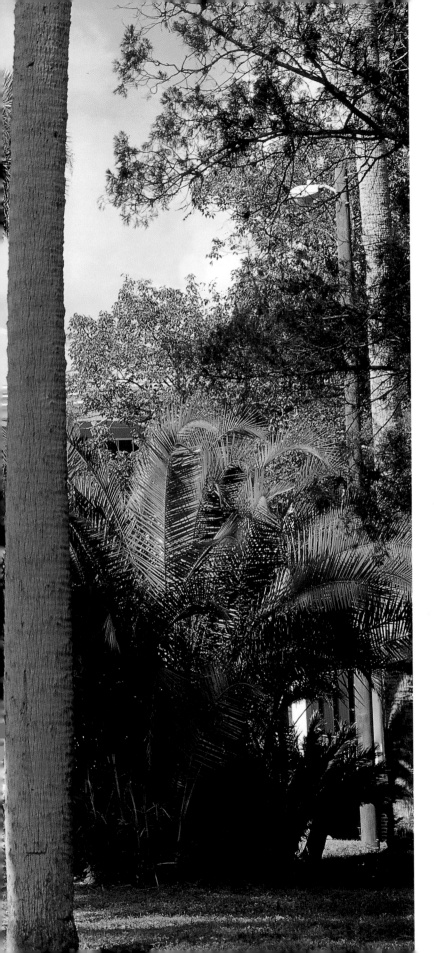

DeBARY HALL, DeBARY

Once the winter home of Samuel Frederick DeBary, an importer of Mumm's champagne and fine French wines, DeBary Hall held many parties and even more guests. The guests arrived by steamboat and often stayed for months, enjoying free-flowing champagne, a spring-fed swimming pool, and game hunting.

DeBary Hall, DeBary

HAWAIIAN FALLS MINIATURE GOLF
DAYTONA BEACH

Hawaiian Falls, the oldest miniature golf attraction in the area, reflects the fun-loving free spirit of Daytona Beach tourism, first brought by Henry Flagler's railroad in 1886. Since the early twentieth century the car has been central to the area's culture, and Daytona Beach is home to many popular roadside attractions, highway diversions, drive-in motels, and even a drive-in church.

Hawaiian Falls Miniature Golf, Daytona Beach

These vintage beachfront tourist cabins, built in 1939, appealed to families traveling by car, who enjoyed the amenities of outdoor barbecues, picnic tables, and proximity to the beach. Daytona's wide white-sand beaches have long drawn admirers. In the 1930s and 1940s, as engineers sought to develop better automobile engines, they conducted land-speed record trials on Daytona's wide densely packed sand beaches—races that became the precursor to the Daytona 500.

Palm Circle Villas, Daytona Beach

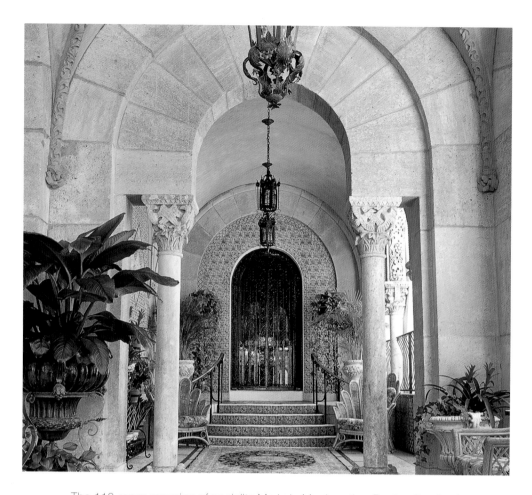

The 118-room mansion of socialite Marjorie Merriweather Post epitomized
Palm Beach glamour for many years. The house, constructed of imported Italian stone,
was designed by architect Marion Syms Wyeth with interiors by Joseph Urban.
Urban, who created opulent sets for Florenz Ziegfeld productions such as *Showboat*,
was known for his exacting eye and dramatic flair. At Mar-a-Lago ("sea to lake"),
Post and her second husband, E. F. Hutton, hosted innumerable lavish parties
with guests ranging from Errol Flynn to British royalty.

The tiled and arched doorway at one end of the ground-floor patio leads to
Mrs. Post's private quarters. Mrs. Post lived at Mar-a-Lago until her death in 1973.

Right: Two stonemasons, a father and son named Franz and Walter Barwig,
lived on the property for four years during construction and executed all of
the stonework. The project required six boatloads of Dorian stone from Italy.
The stonework as seen in this courtyard was conceived to suggest an aviary.
Carved birds decorate surfaces such as archways and Corinthian columns.

One end of the thirty-four-foot-high living room, originally called the "party room," is dominated by an enormous fireplace with the Post family crest at its center. The large wooden doors are covered in gold-leafed cherubs. Local legend has it that during Mar-a-Lago's construction in the 1920s, the state of Florida ran out of gold leaf, and the estate's head gilder was forced to travel to Europe to buy more.

Mar-a-Lago, Palm Beach

A spiral staircase leads up to the Seven Windows Room, which was used as a sleeping porch. The repeating falconer motif on the ceiling evokes its medieval status as a symbol of the leisure class—as well as the Posts' own falcons.

Mar-a-Lago, Palm Beach

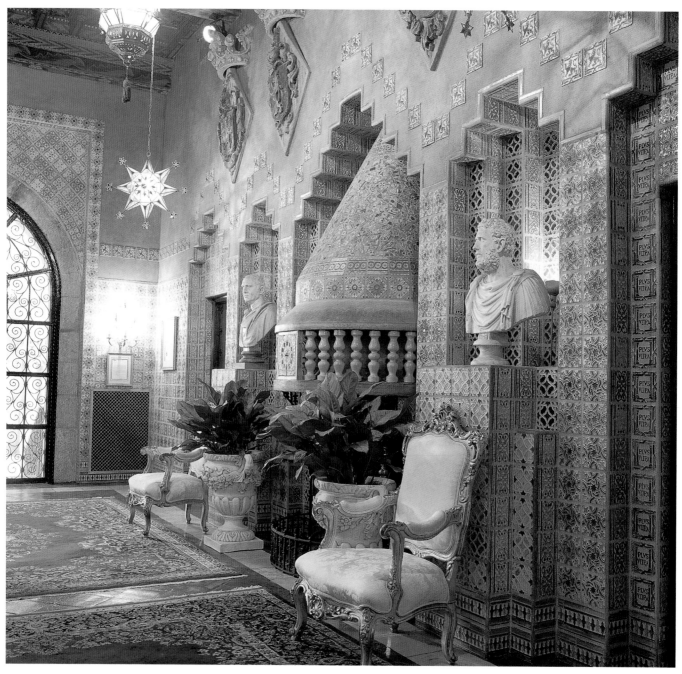

132

Exotic light fixtures greet visitors in the reception hall. The tiles come from a Spanish collection of thirty-six thousand tiles, dating back as far as the sixteenth century, bought for Mrs. Post by a scout. Mrs. Post had a network of people all over the world searching for fantastic and ancient architectural elements to incorporate into her home.

Mar-a-Lago, Palm Beach

Colorful beachfront cabanas in front of the house offered guests private places for changing into swimsuits. Post bequeathed Mar-a-Lago to the federal government as a winter White House, but the government couldn't manage the $3 million annual maintenance budget and put the estate up for sale. Donald Trump bought it in 1985 and reopened it ten years later as a private club.

Mar-a-Lago, Palm Beach

134

This simple cottage was home to writer Laura (Riding) Jackson from the early 1940s
until her death in 1991. She and her husband, Schuyler B. Jackson,
raised organic citrus here. The structure was moved from nearby Wabasso, Florida,
in 1994 to be preserved as an excellent example of vernacular Cracker architecture.
Laura was a well-regarded modernist poet in the 1920s and 1930s,
and was awarded the prestigious Bollingen prize in 1991. However,
when she married Jackson she renounced poetry and they devoted themselves
to creating a new, more direct English-language dictionary.

Right: The small-frame building is made of locally milled Florida pine.
Laura's apron hangs on the kitchen door.

Laura (Riding) Jackson House, Vero Beach

The house is furnished today with Laura (Riding) Jackson's belongings, including her typewriter and her dictionary. Laura and her husband lived here simply as they worked on their comprehensive study of language, which she completed after her husband's death. *A New Foundation for the Definition of Words* expresses their belief that language is the key to problems between individuals and nations, and that an English dictionary with clear definitions would ease much of the world's unhappiness.

The bedroom opens out onto the island view. In her later years, Riding would often write from the bed itself. About her life in Wabasso she said, "My husband and I were let be—left alone to be, left alone to do—by the Floridian version of the nature of nature, which I think, is, in its essential universality, to let be and let do."

Laura (Riding) Jackson House, Vero Beach

138

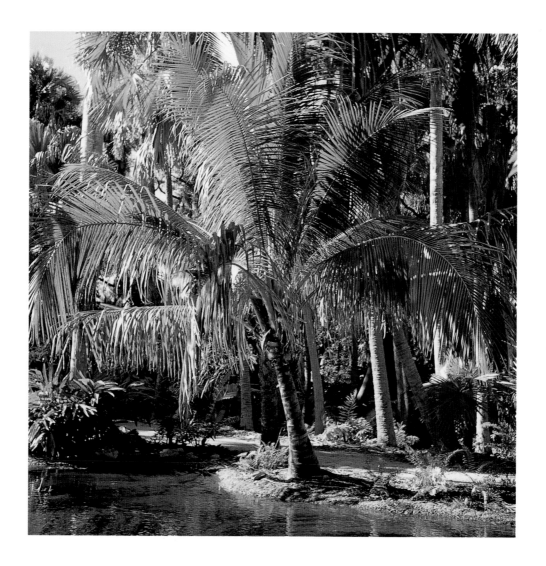

During the Depression, Waldo Sexton, an eccentric and prolific local builder,
and Arthur McKee, a Cleveland industrialist, set out to preserve eighty acres of tropical
landscape. The original McKee Jungle Gardens (later renamed the McKee Botanical
Garden) was soon expanded to include an excellent collection of waterlilies and orchids.
They hired William Lyman Phillips—partner in the firm of Frederick Law Olmsted, Jr.—to
create a master plan for the property. Over the years, the plant collection was constantly
enlarged by their friend David Fairchild, a plant explorer for the USDA.

McKee Botanical Garden, Vero Beach

The Hall of Giants was designed in the style of a Polynesian ceremonial palace. It is festooned with bells from Sexton's collection, gathered from ships, trains, and civic buildings.

McKee Botanical Garden, Vero Beach

The recently restored Hall of Giants is a board-and-batten building constructed of cypress and heart pine logs. With no formal architectural training, Waldo Sexton designed the building to hold the world's largest one-piece mahogany table. Sexton was a legendary collector. He frequented Palm Beach auctions during the distress sales of the Depression, when mansions and warehouses were being emptied, and paid cash for pieces to furnish his buildings around town.

McKee Botanical Garden, Vero Beach

The Spanish Kitchen at the McKee Botanical Garden was a large outdoor barbecue area with enough grilling space to grill one hundred steaks at a time, along with large iron kettles for potatoes and swamp cabbage—the favorite meal of gardens cofounder Waldo Sexton.

McKee Botanical Garden, Vero Beach

Right: An old orange grove at twilight captures the essence of old Florida.
Merritt Island is where Captain Douglas Dummit developed the famous Indian River Oranges
in the mid-nineteenth century from seedling stock originally brought to Florida by the Spanish.

144

On Merritt Island some small family-run groves still sell their oranges at roadside stands.

Merritt Island

In a tidy trailer park near Cape Canaveral, this vintage streamlined aluminum 1950s model, with the optimistic name "Spartan Executive Mansion," looks decidedly less mobile than its designer might have foreseen. Owners of such trailers were originally called "tin can tourists," but many of them came to stay, settling in for good.

Cape Canaveral

Built in 1921, the waterfront Bonnet House was home to Frederic Bartlett and
Helen Birch Bartlett, natives of Chicago. (After Helen died in 1925, Frederic remarried and
shared the house with Evelyn Fortune Lilly.) Frederic, an artist, designed the house,
which is named for the yellow Bonnet lilies that grow on the thirty-five-acre property.
Helen's father had first acquired the site that the house sits on and much surrounding
land after blowing ashore at Fort Lauderdale during a sudden Atlantic storm;
he felt divine intervention had brought him to the area.

The entrance to the house's inner courtyard sits in a "desert garden" planted with
yucca, palmetto, century plants, and unusual trees. A carved fish sits above the door.
Evelyn Bartlett later recalled that her husband "did have a sense of whimsy."

Right: Theatrical accents define the living room at Bonnet House. Evelyn, like
her husband, was an artist and loved color. The gilded Baroque columns around
the door, the diamond-pattern tile floor, and the mahogany ceiling suggest
the couple's creative lifestyle. Frederic's paintings adorn the walls.

The Shell Museum is a separate building on the property. It adjoins an orchid house and a bamboo-lined cocktail bar. Frederic designed the small museum as a gift for Evelyn and combined within it her favorite things: orchids, shells, and socializing with friends. When entertaining, the couple often served cocktails in this space before moving outside to the courtyard for dinner.

152

On the ceiling of the north loggia Frederic painted a mountainous shoreline, with fish, shells, and a turtle.
Evelyn added a large net to complete the scene. Beyond the doors lies the dining room,
which is decorated with mounted fish caught by the Bartletts.

Bonnet House, Fort Lauderdale

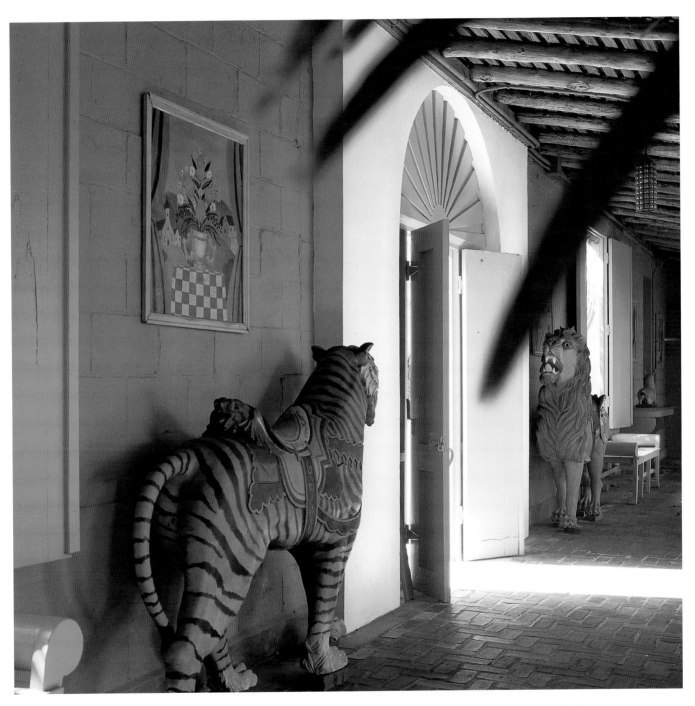

153

The house's courtyard is ringed with an open loggia that provides a natural breezeway for the dining and drawing rooms. Carousel animals are found around the loggia.

Both Frederic and Evelyn painted in this enormous studio, and Frederic's paintings still hang throughout the room. Frederic had trained in Munich and studied with James McNeill Whistler. Frederic and Helen also built an important collection of post-impressionist paintings, including works by Seurat, Matisse, Van Gogh, Cézanne, and Gaugin, which were donated to the Art Institute of Chicago

Bonnet House, Fort Lauderdale

VIZCAYA MUSEUM AND GARDENS
MIAMI

Inspired by a villa near Venice, Vizcaya was the winter home of James Deering, son of the developer of the Deering Harvest Machine. The estate, which also included a dairy farm, poultry house, stable, greenhouse, and staff residences, was designed by three architects: F. Burrall Hoffman designed the buildings, Diego Suarez created the gardens, and Paul Chalfin directed the overall vision. Its construction required the labor of one thousand workers for two years, from 1914 to 1916. Deering had first envisioned a more modest residence, asking "must we be so grand?" But Chalfin persuaded him to dream on a larger scale.

156

Vizcaya Museum and Gardens, Miami

Between the house and the Bay of Biscayne, the ornamental "Stone Barge" was used for lavish parties and as a breakwater. The striped gondola pole in the foreground is on the dock where Deering tied his yacht, the "Nepenthe."

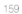

Vizcaya Museum and Gardens, Miami

160

Shell-lined grottoes near the water are protected by giant stone sculptures.
Inside, shade and fountains provide a respite from the sun.

Vizcaya's ten acres of Italianate gardens include obelisks, urns, and marble busts among the plantings. Clipped oaks stand at the edge of the reflecting pool. The gardens were not completed until 1921, five years after the house, because of World War I.

The grand swimming pool lies both inside and outside the house. The ceiling of the pool house is covered with dolphins.

Vizcaya Museum and Gardens, Miami

In the tradition of formal Italian gardens, the landscape design at Vizcaya was conceived by architect Diego Suarez as an "outdoor room."

165

Vizcaya Museum and Gardens, Miami

Vizcaya is laid out around a central courtyard
with arcades such as this one on three sides.
Stuccoed concrete is the primary building material,
with native coral stone for trim around windows and doors.

Vizcaya Museum and Gardens, Miami

Miami Beach's Raleigh Hotel is one of the city's Art Deco gems. Designed by noted architect Lawrence Murray Dixon, the hotel opened in 1940. Throughout the 1930s and 1940s Dixon designed many of Miami Beach's Art Deco hotels, houses, and businesses.

Raleigh Hotel, Miami Beach

Contrasting bands of wood paneling lend the Raleigh's dining room a clean, modern air. At a white-tie ball on the hotel's opening night, an unknown Desi Arnaz was discovered when he filled in for a sick bandmember.

Raleigh Hotel, Miami Beach

Esther Williams filmed many of her famous
swimming scenes in the Raleigh's curvaceous pool.

Raleigh Hotel, Miami Beach

THE BARBARA APARTMENTS
MIAMI BEACH

The Barbara—with its sleek horizontal bands, called "speed lines," and rounded corners—represents the Streamlined Moderne style popular at the end of the Art Deco era. Streamlined buildings eschewed surface decoration and harsh angular elevations.

The Barbara Apartments, Miami Beach

CHARLES DEERING ESTATE, MIAMI

Built by Charles Deering—brother of James, whose home Vizcaya is nearby—
this home is known as the "Stone House." The Mediterranean Revival–style house was
inspired by the castles Deering owned in Spain. Note the inlaid shells
on the porch's shallow barrel vault.

Charles Deering Estate, Miami

The lobby of the Indian Creek Hotel was originally furnished by the celebrated designer Norman Bel Geddes in 1936. The water pitchers on the mantel were placed in each room for the guests' refreshment.

176

Glen Curtiss, a former pilot turned urban developer, created the planned town of Opa-Locka in North Miami Dade County to evoke an "Arabian fantasy" based on the book *1001 Tales of the Arabian Nights*. Streets were laid out in Moorish crescent patterns, and the multi-domed City Hall was the community's centerpiece. Pink stripes, pink domes, minarets, and giant pink urns link the 1920s building to Miami's famed Art Deco tradition.

City Hall, Opa-Locka

CORAL CASTLE, HOMESTEAD

Working alone and often at night, a slight man named Edward Leedskalnin built the Coral Castle over thirty years, beginning in 1920. He sculpted a castle, a surrounding defensive wall, and a large sculpture garden on ten acres. How he single-handedly worked and moved enormous blocks of coral, which weighs approximately 125 pounds per cubic foot, remains a mystery.

In the center of the property, in a quiet spot where Ed liked to read, is a group of tables and chairs.

Coral Castle, Homestead

Sections of the massive coral wall are eight feet tall, four feet wide, and three feet thick, and weigh more than six tons. Ed's feat has astonished and puzzled scientists and engineers. Some of the pieces that he quarried—all of the coral came from his property—weighed more than twenty-eight tons. He began the project after being rejected by the love of his life, Agnes Scuffs, whom he always called "Sweet Sixteen," after her age at the time he knew her.

following pages:
In one corner of the site stand several sculptural forms. The "moon pond" shows the three phases of the moon. The planets Mars and Saturn are close by. Concentric circles represent the solar system. The Coral Castle has been placed on the National Register of Historic Places.

Coral Castle, Homestead

LA PALMA RESTAURANT, CORAL GABLES

George Edgar Merrick developed Coral Gables, a
Mediterranean-style section of Miami, in the 1920s.
He was heavily influenced by the City Beautiful movement
popular in the early twentieth century, which promoted
tree-lined streets, lush parks, winding roadways, and
handsome lampposts. Merrick and his partners added to
these principles a Mediterranean flair, with fountains,
plazas, and Spanish street names.

186

The arched gates to Coral Gables were designed to mark the border with greater Miami and purposely recall triumphal gates in Spanish cities.

Coral Gables

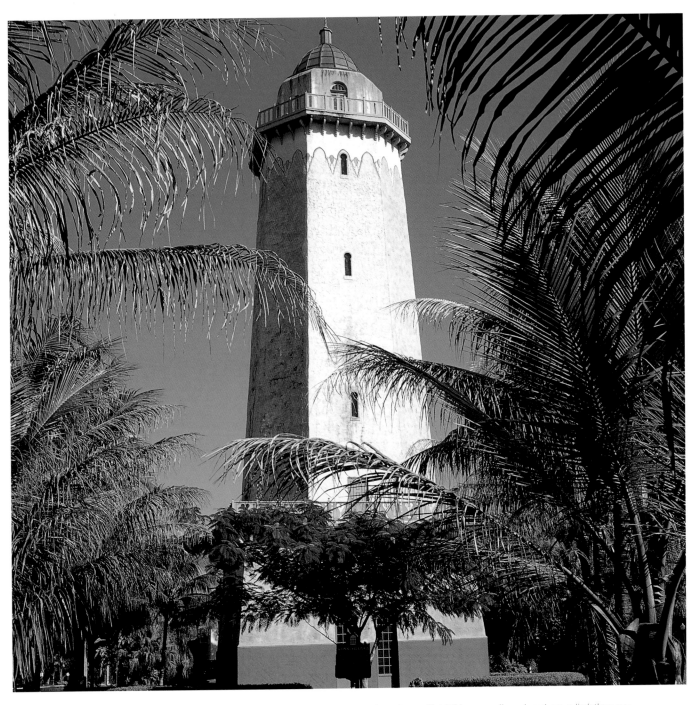

The water tower in Coral Gables, which provided water to the city until 1931, was disguised as a lighthouse. Once altered, it is now restored to its original state.

left: The Coral Gables Congregational Church—one of the community's earliest religious structures—is a replica of a church in Costa Rica. The baroque belfry and façade embellishments are true to the original.

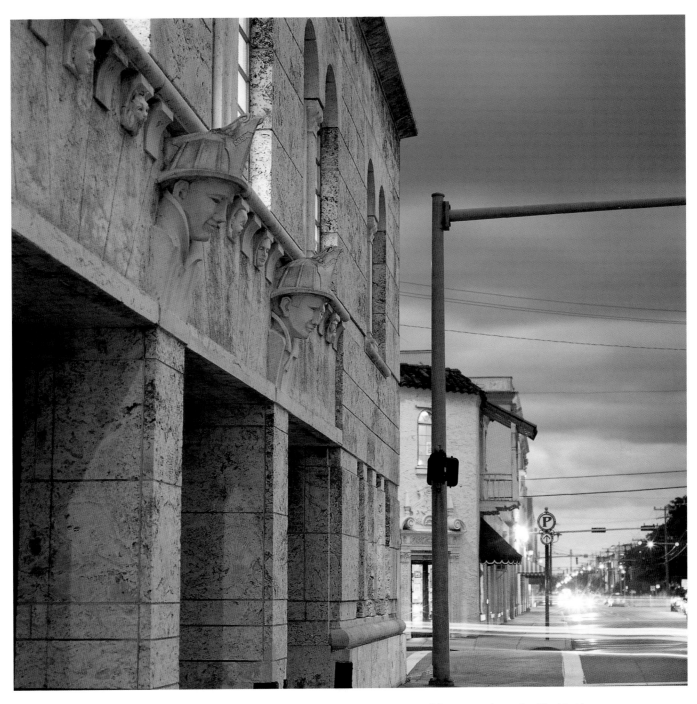

The Depression Moderne police and fire station, built in 1939 of limestone from the Florida Keys, features sculptures of firemen's heads on the front of the building.

THE BILTMORE HOTEL, CORAL GABLES

The stunning Biltmore Hotel was the centerpiece of
Merrick's plan for Coral Gables. This luxury resort hotel was
designed by the New York architectural firm of Schultze and
Weaver, who also created New York City's Waldorf-Astoria,
and opened in 1926. The lobby reveals the building's
Mediterranean Revival style and grand scale.

The Biltmore Hotel, Coral Gables

The Biltmore included multiple courtyards, such as this one, a country club, canals, gardens, and a golf course. During World War II, it served as an Army hospital, but it has since been restored to its former glory.

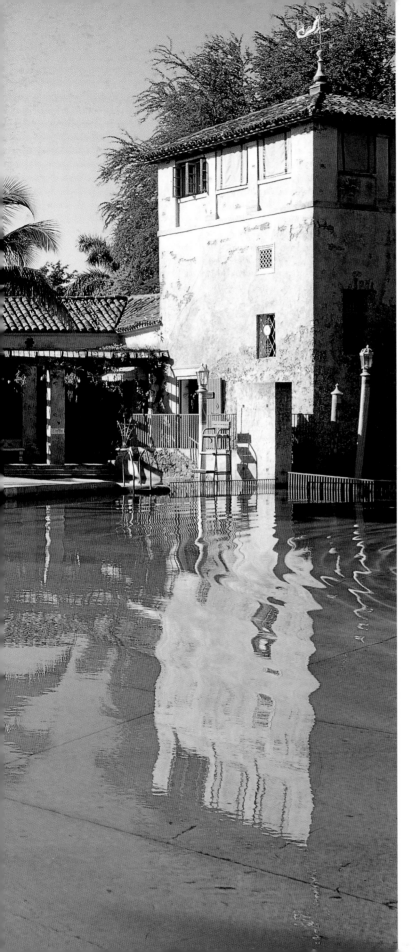

VENETIAN POOL, CORAL GABLES

The elegant Venetian Pool, fed by cool underground springs and complemented with loggias, porticoes, bridges, and waterfalls, was once a lowly quarry pit. George Merrick and architect Phineas Paist transformed it into what appears to be a natural lagoon in Venice. The beautiful blue-green water is drained every night and refilled from the springs.

195

Venetian Pool, Coral Gables

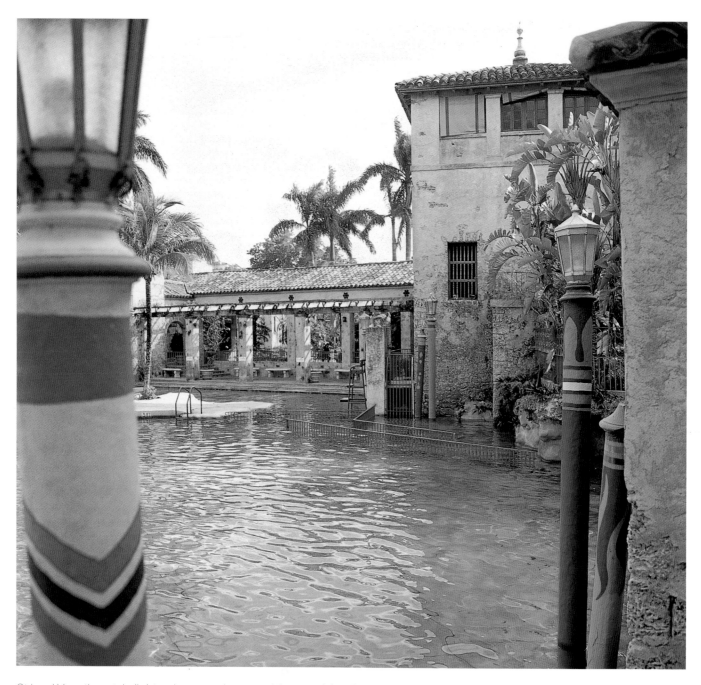

Striped Venetian-style light poles complemented the gondolas that once traversed the "world's most beautiful swimming hole."
In its heyday, the pool drew Miami's most glamorous people. Beauty contests were held on specially constructed
platforms, and Esther Williams and Johnny Weismuller swam the pool's length. Swimmers can explore grottoes
and waterfalls or cross bridges to floating islands complete with palm trees.

Venetian Pool, Coral Gables

BARNACLE HOUSE, COCONUT GROVE

The oldest house still in its original location in Dade County, Barnacle House was built in 1891. A naval architect named Ralph Middleton Munroe moved to Florida with his wife, who had been diagnosed with tuberculosis, and in 1886 purchased the property on which the house now sits. Although his wife died before the house was finished, Munroe persisted. The structure began as a simple, one-story bungalow on wood pilings with an octagonal room at its center. The room's shape, which tapers off to an open-air vent, reminded Munroe of a barnacle and gave the home its name. Munroe remarried and eventually expanded the house by raising the original structure to become the second floor and creating a new ground floor below.

Privacy was ensured by the hardwood forest "hammock" between the road and the house, through which Munroe cleared a path just wide enough for one buggy.

Barnacle House, Coconut Grove

Munroe designed the central room of the house as an octagon because of the shape's structural strength in the face of strong winds. The house incurred only minimal damage during the great hurricane of 1926 and Hurricane Andrew of 1992. In the original, one-story house, this space was the dining room, and the gingerbread upper gallery dates from that period.

Barnacle House, Coconut Grove

200

The living room fireplace was embellished by Munroe's son, Wirth Munroe.
He shaped the mantel out of solid mahogany and the surround out of coral. Wirth lived in the house until his death in 1969.

Barnacle House, Coconut Grove

This pine-paneled bedroom belonged to Ralph Munroe's oldest daughter, Patty, until she married.
It opens onto the second-story front porch. In one of Monroe's many nautical touches, he framed the house with
lumber legally salvaged from shipwrecks along Florida's reef.

Barnacle House, Coconut Grove

The kitchen of Barnacle House was expanded after the 1926 hurricane and outfitted with modern plumbing and an electric refrigerator.

Barnacle House, Coconut Grove

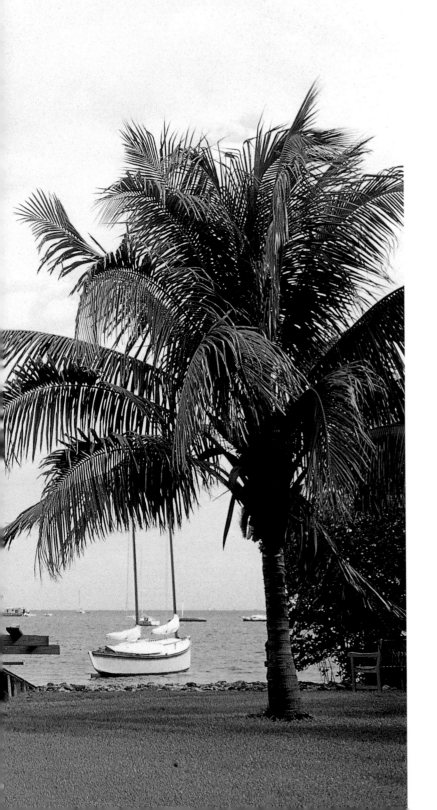

The simple boathouse looks out on Key Biscayne. It was the first structure on the site, built in 1887, and Munroe lived in it while the main house was being constructed. Munroe took great pleasure in designing yachts and was commodore of the Biscayne Bay Yacht Club for twenty-two years after its formation in 1887.

Key Biscayne

Resources

The following historical sites are open to the public:

Barnacle House, Coconut Grove
(305) 448-9445
www.abfla.com/parks/Barnacle.html

The Bok Sanctuary, Lake Wales
(863) 676-1408
www.boksanctuary.org

Bonnet House, Fort Lauderdale
(954) 563-5393
www.bonnethouse.org

Ca d'Zan, Ringling Museum of Art, Sarasota
(941) 359-5700
www.ringling.org

Cigar Worker's Casita, Ybor City Museum State Park, Tampa
(813) 247-6323
www.ybormuseum.org

The Coral Castle, Homestead
(305) 248-6345
www.coralcastle.com

DeBary Hall, DeBary
(386) 668-3840

The Deering Estate, at Cutler, Miami
(305) 235-1668
www.metro-dade.com/parks/deering.htm

Edison Winter Estate, Fort Myers
(239) 334-7419
www.edison-ford-estate.com

Gamble Place at Spruce Creek Preserve, Port Orange
(386) 255-0285
www.moas.org

González-Alvarez House, St. Augustine
(904) 824-2872
www.oldcity.com/oldhouse

The Laura (Riding) Jackson House, Vero Beach
(561) 589-6711
www.lauraridingjackson.org

Kingsley Plantation, Fort George Island, Jacksonville
(904) 251-3537

Koreshan Unity Settlement, Estero
(239) 992-0311

McKee Botanical Gardens, Vero Beach
(772) 794-0601
www.mckeegarden.org

Henry B. Plant Museum, Tampa
(813) 254-1891
www.plantmuseum.com

Marjorie Kinnan Rawlings House, Hawthorne
(352) 466-3672
www.marjoriekinnanrawlings.org

Smallwood Store, Chokoloskee Island
(239) 695-2989
www.florida-everglades.com/chokol/smallw.htm

St. Augustine Alligator Farm, St. Augustine
www.alligatorfarm.com

St. Augustine Lighthouse & Museum, St. Augustine
(904) 829-0745
www.staugustinelighthouse.com

Sunken Gardens, St. Petersburg
(727) 551-3100
www.stpete.org/sunken.htm

Tampa Theatre, Tampa
(813) 274-8286
www.tampatheatre.org

Venetian Pool, Coral Gables
(305) 460-5356
www.venetianpool.com

Vizcaya Museum and Gardens, Miami
(305) 250-9133
www.vizcayamuseum.com

Ximenez-Fatio House, St. Augustine
(904) 829-3575
http://www.oldcity.com/ximenez/index.html

Left: One of two "Blue Mist Ladies" from the Blue Mist Motel, a themed beachfront motel in Sunny Isles Beach.

Acknowledgments

Many thanks to the following people who helped us produce this book:

Anne Daley
Bernard Mayer
Rick Esposito
Richard Warholic
Joe Pescarino
Ed Mintiens
L.T.I. Lab, NYC & Miami
Edith & Ernest Gross
Nicholas Gross
Peter Fodera
Ken Needleman
Jim & Betty Daley
Jennie & Bruce Chastain
Dr. Mabel Ginsburg
Theresa Ward
Chris Ludlam
Rob Tate
Terence McArdle at Kodak

and especially our book designers
Judy Geib & Aldo Sampieri

and our editor Alex Tart